Societies Acquaintance

(its not what it seems)

this book is dedicated to a person i no longer call friend.

thank you for inspiring me and reminding me you are just another piece of society.

CONTENTS

unhealthy cravings..........................3
the confessions of a time-waster..4
the blade's guilt..5
why bitterness?...6
unifinished business..7
the fair game won you a prize..8
familiar monster..9
to kill a partner...10
used book part one..11
used book part two..12
origins...13
the guilty survivor..14
why do people think i'm crazy?..15
the virgin...16
promises you can't keep..17
aphrodite's apprentice..18
the bird that couldn't fly..19
thief of verity...20
same old mistakes..21
vulture of discretion..22
woman...23
young...24
impenetrable door..25
at peace...26
chasing...27
simple and pure..28
the curse...29
the hated victim..30
memories of a lost vaction..31
irony..32
the brutal truth..33
society...34

unhealthy cravings

like the sun, you're the first one i feel
through my little bedroom window when I wake up in the morning.
but also what I crave when at night you go away leaving nothing but a silver sphere of emptiness
I can't help but close my eyes in hopes ill feel you again when the morning comes

the confessions of a time-waster

sixteen and sad, waiting for seventeen
seventeen and filled with lost hope, waiting for eighteen maybe I won't mope
eighteen and lost
why did you leave again?
I promise it won't cost
cost you nothing just to be here
don't just disappear
you make me feel like I'm sixteen again
sixteen and sad
why are you so disastrous
you give me faith
you make me feel like I'm seventeen again
seventeen and in despair
I think I will mope
I'm eighteen and lost
yes I need you
why did I believe you

the blade's guilt

we loved so deeply
deep like a blade cutting soft skin
the blood serves as the effort we put in
i bled out, but you still had blood to spare

why bitterness?
the concept of love is hard to understand. you can love a stranger
a foreign soul to your nature
yet you can loathe someone you know
someone who has been imprisoned
in the cages of your heart.

unfinished business

what gives it the right to walk away
with a part of me when I'm still trying to piece your parts together?
I gave you everything
you gave me broken parts
broken parts I learned to love
but you still couldn't love me
for all of my complete and pieced parts.

the fair game won you a prize

do you really love me?
am I the first thing you think of in the morning and the last at night?
does the art you indulge in have little fragments of me in it?
is two seconds without me the same as two long bleak months?
the sound of my not-so-perfect voice turns your bad day into a good one?
when we touch does the pit in your stomach fill with a dozen butterflies?
do you really love me?
or am I just a phase?
or am I just a meaningless prize at a fair?
maybe it's the sexual things we do that you love?
maybe it's just my body?
now I know the truth
you don't love me
you love how easily it took me to love you.
congratulations
you won.

familiar monster

you watch the little girl laugh and smile.
she grins as she plays with her many dolls.
she is beautiful
so young
so innocent
she isn't smiling anymore
she's crossing her arms whenever you come to the family dinners
but she isn't cold.
she isn't smiling anymore when you place a soft but desperate knock at her pink wooden door at the entrance of her room.

now the little girl wasn't little anymore,
she's grown up in your eyes, she's just fifteen
you think she doesn't act her age, so you tell her how mature she is.
does anyone know what you think?
what you do to her when no one is around?

the little girl isn't little anymore
she has her own car
the keys to her own apartment
the door is white now, it has no invitation to be opened
she isn't scared anymore
she knows your secret
your dirty little secret.
and she's coming for you.

to kill a partner
in this story we are unlikely
our dance is a rough one
we twist and turn in the sole
purpose of making one another
fall.

but when we lose balance
somehow our hands intertwine
helping each other get back up

the fall is destructive
and every time we stand
back on our feet, we come
back with a different wound
a different pain or scar

this dancing comes
with consequences
consequences we both have
no mind in enduring
until we can't dance anymore

used book part one

I know how this story ends
the pages of this book have been read
they have been flipped countless times
I've memorized the page numbers
dried tears are still imprinted in chapter 16
its spine is fragile and unstable
its pages are wounded, scarred, and ripped
it has been consumed by my bitter touch
yet I still come back to it
the comfort of knowing how the story ends
that is what pulls me back to it each time
I know our ending
but yet I still choose to read it.

used book part two

my hand hesitates as it reaches for the blank wordless book
its touch feels foreign
its course is almost unreadable
a book with no story, no flaws, no mistakes
a new story, a new beginning
the ending of this story is something I have no knowledge of
is it like the last one?
I'm scared, terrified to open its pages
picking up the pen I begin writing our story
our story that I do not know the ending of

origins
you feel invisible
so speak
because your silence
isn't worth their pride

the guilty survivor
the cuts in your heart are relics
reminders that you have been
brave enough throughout your silent battles
while others lacked the courage to fight

I love you is a foreign word in your book
of spoken truths
when thinking of forever you think of
the end

your first heartbreak
love you didn't receive from your family
the love that is supposed to be
absolute
indestructible
expecting disappointment from love
became easier than it should be

you feel like a fraud
telling others to be strong
that everything will eventually get better
when you are so close to crumbling
you realize the only person who
needs the advice
is yourself
do you take it?

why do people think i'm crazy?
peace is boredom to you
because you have grown up in the chaos
a burning house
in which the wood enjoys the fire.

the virgin

why must everything be so confusing in a
a universe where right and wrong aren't known?
should we have done it this way?
it felt right
I think that is how it was supposed to feel
you don't talk to me anymore
did I do something wrong?
we can do it again
i promise this time i won't protest
this time it will be something i won't detest

promises you can't keep

if this earth is to keep us apart
the one promise I can bestow you is
I will never cease to search for you

in the gazes of the crowds I pass by
in the melody of soft tunes
or in the grave where you lie sleeping
I will search for you on the other side
the only thing that plunged was my knife

aphrodite's apprentice

In society's handbook, I'm far from perfect
in the eyes of my mother, I have potential
the words of my friends reassure me of the beauty I am blind to see
in the mirror that sits before me, I can't help but question what is true
it whispers cruel remarks to me
Its fragile arms enfold me with tenderness in moments of strength
most of the time I attempt to avoid confronting its gaze
I never know what it's reaching to tell me
the imperfect curves of my body are chiseled by the gods - they say
Aphrodite's fingertips slide softly through the side of my cheek
she ensures me my grace
nobody is perfect child, she says
yet I still crave the flawless figure I am expected to possess
who am I truly, I ask Venus
when will the small voice in my head that becomes louder everyday stop its protests
she simply smiles with empathy
her golden essence imprisons me
the goddess of love is teaching me slowly
that the most powerful love should be
felt for one's self.

the bird that couldn't fly

fly away you mumbled
but how can i fly
if you have cut my wings?
you don't want to see me cry
yet you take pleasure in tugging my strings

thief of verity
what you see is my disguise
the beauty that lies outside
to see inside all you have to do is ask
you prefer what is easy to perceive
if you cared enough you would see
inside is the beauty you thieve

same old mistakes
these sad songs are way overdue
to heal the pain you put me through
what you did was unforgivable
i can’t help but think i'm invincible
going back to you is so typical

vulture of discretion

just lose five more pounds
then you can fit in that dress
ten pounds I assure you
with that boy, it won't be a stress
maybe fifteen more will do you good
you look great
it just needs a little shaping
gone with all the weight
now you say ill get a date
don't you see I'm slipping away?
all my insecurities in display
you pick them one by one
to see which one you'll get to prey

woman

it's way too late to be out
will anybody hear me if i shout?
my hoodie and sweatpants will surely bring no attention
attracting interest is not my intention
the light of my phone is my guide
yet it doesn't stop the demise
i just wanted to go home
now i lay here on the cold concrete floor
my clothes are no longer on me
you have taken something from me
all i wanted was to go home

young

it's slowly building itself
it's not easy to mold
not perfect for sure
some parts are cold
both of us so immature
for our love is new
the experience we have is few
you'll hurt me in the end
on you i will always depend

impenetrable door

my heart will forever belong to you
whispers of apologies
your embrace enveloping me again
my eyes never leave the door you walked out from
the door you would come in from so often
the door is now closed
but you’re not waiting for me on the other side

at peace

i love you isn't enough
i've started to love you more than everything
songs aren't as beautiful as the sound of your voice
i have learned to love you more than the ocean by choice
the water doesn't glisten the same as your eyes do
your comfort is the only thing i want to pursue
i love you is a word we don't need to say to each other no longer

chasing
clinginess creates imaginary affections
clinging onto an idea rather than a reality

simple and pure
silence turned into comfort

the curse
the forgiving heart
it believes in the people it shouldn't
forgives those who have shattered it
it allows the suffering to resurface
with open arms, it will accept those who have wronged it to return
until the heart can't take it anymore
until the people who have stepped on it have severed it perpetually
that is when the forgiving heart turns into something else
it has nothing to offer because it will never trust again.

the hated victim
there's a difference between us
you lied to make people hate me
i lied to make people like you
now you lie alone
and i lie surrounded by the people you tried to persuade
because in spite of everything, your true colors will never be hidden by the lies i created to shield them

memories of a lost vacation
you ran the red lights that i set between us
the blame was on me as you crashed the car
i wasn’t the one driving
i was just a passenger
as your voyage came to an end
i was dropped off
your memory of me faltered
you drove back home in search of a new place to visit

irony
you never apologized for how you treated me
but, you blamed me for how i reacted

the brutal truth

"i never loved you"
your face numb as you looked at me
there was no regret in that confession
a brutal truth that i convinced myself to be a lie
a strategy
my vision became foggy as my eyes
connected with yours
your dry, emotionless eyes
the same eyes that once begged for my company

society

"keep your friends close but enemies closer"
surrounding yourself with those you hate
is that the company you want to keep?
or is that just society in your ear whispering demands?
we are told what to do by others but never think of our own needs
society has an influence in all of us
society is the keep close
while the friend you push away
is yourself

www.ingramcontent.com/pod-product-compliance
Lightning Source LLC
LaVergne TN
LVHW052112160826
845678LV00015B/3511
9798847896580